Fawn in the light

Desirae S

BookLeaf Publishing

India | USA | UK

Presentation by *BookLeaf Publishing*

Web: www.bookleafpub.com

E-mail: info@bookleafpub.com

ISBN: 9789357215282

First edition 2022

*I want to thank God, my family and to those
that form their words into everyday poetry,
Thank you!*

ACKNOWLEDGEMENT

I want to show recognition to those that have been a part of my journey in any way and those that will be, including you reading now.

I want to give sincere appreciation for the adverse moments as they led me to search the isolated wilderness for strength to survive while I continued to beautify some of the darkest times in my life.

I want to display the deepest gratitude wholeheartedly to the ones who listen without judgment and spoke positivity into me when I needed it the most.

PREFACE

Determined from a young age, replaying in my mind like a broken record was to break the cycle. This set me on a long journey of healing and continued healing from Trauma, PTSD, Anxiety and Addiction leading to the collection in this book.

Makes you

This life takes courage
Take the sacrifice
Choose what you do, choice
Do it bold, be valiant
To love what you do, daring
But love is strength
Take the sacrifice
Control your thoughts, be positive
Make your life happy

Insanity Smile

Now here you are irrational
You developed lunacy
a meaningful delusion
Your voice mania
express incoherent
no tolerance for folly
closing the door on delirium
for it is neurosis
But you are completely mad!

Tragedy Scream

Misfortune of being prey
a catastrophe that cursed her
deep affliction of self love
the wreck they each left her in silenced with
stilling pain
because you are a liar,
that is not something we discuss,
Impending doom with continued adversity, the
only way through
is the death of her silence
Shook her free from that childhood neighbor,
that step-cousin, that brother in-law, that date

Point of view

Reaching inside myself to give you a viewpoint
You reached a vista
Context for the scene that changed everything
comes later
The current scenery a broad valley leading to
higher ground
But if you view the panorama
The angle of his sword was
Killing me

Lost Soul

5

Mourning little me
Lacking love
In need of stability
Left in destitute
Cost of addiction
Deep grief for trauma took me
Waste of tears on old sorrow
Defeat inevitable
Thrive through it

Captive Spirit

Pleasure a prison
Bondage to pain
Rape the imprisonment
Caged memory
Hostage in freeze response
Bound to a moment unfree
Truth refusing to pay the ransom
For her release

11:30

You live in isolation
You survive in seclusion
Monotony has built the walls,
to silence the ache
The empty quiet, longing to feel
Vulnerability, seen as frail
Lack no excuses
No vice goes alone
Debility
Feeble attempt to fix shortcomings
Folly a incurable disease
Live clear
Be gently vigilant of emotions
Let them rise
You are brave
Relearn
Vulnerability is strength

Linger

Can it be just,
assault lives in memory
Where eyes can't close off the attack
You survived the injury
brutality of a soul
Can it be just,
PTSD is part of your tumult horizon
Where eyes can't close off the aggression
brutality of a soul
where eyes can't see
endured pain,
brutality of a soul
You survived

Greif heard

Tears of anguish for the girl silenced
When she finally feels the loss and all around
her sorrow
She struggles with heartache trying to recapture
security
Left in lament and woe
Just wanting to have a voice
Emerging on the other side of healing bereaved
of her little self no longer struggling through the
pain she will be heard

Shocked

Paralysis of trauma
Left in a stupor
Numb protection for disbelief
Now a complex wreck
Felt a jolt of truth
A crash in the mind
The spark of healing

Introspection

11

Alone avoidant
Instead of crying
Seeking isolation
Disappearing into seclusion
Vanishing recluse
Emotions are private
Memories remote
Emerge the introvert

Challenge change

12

Somewhere between obstacles and trials was what she survived, at odds with who she was becoming. She was starting to love her moxie. And find comfort in the date of her wildest dreams. She wasn't always this way; she had to persevere. She overcame her entire world

Waves

Shaken from the surge
a wave of bewilderment
swelling to the surface
welcome in anxiety, let's float with ease
Accept it we are going to rise and fall with the
tide
Value our time together, we will get more skilled
Embrace the current

Creativity light

Are we still inventive,
holding on to imagination, in hopes of
originality
Are we still clever,
holding onto vision, in hopes of
talent
Are we still genius,
holding onto light, in hopes of
inspiration

Inventory

15

Change filled with approval
A fortune within
An abundance in not knowing
Value in believing in each other
Find wealth in balance
Rare perspective true gratitude for all
Precious confidence in all things positive
Trove in letting go

Strength now

And so the vitality will grow from the fortitude
you feel
Those muscle memory moments will be the
toughest moments to overcome don't turn back
your pith is astonishing
clarity you feel health with the same heartache
You now understand your power
You developed a potency few can understand

Forgetting fear

There is no award or success to fulfill your soul
needs
but you keep crowning your heart the winner it
triumphs your melancholy
You strive for your heart to make your mind
understand
You must love you first
Handing your heart in oblivion
Co-signing love
Disremember the scorn that came before
Clean slate
Escape fear
Amit insecurities
this heart
It is meant to love

Heart handover

18

Self reliance comes with scars,
Assured weary,
Strength saved for tomorrow,
Confidence put into determination,
Consistency the fuel,
Afraid she gave her heart again,
She knew the risk,
Unsure if it was in danger this time,
She watched aghast,
To the onlookers reaction,
Stricken with panic and fearful for her heart was
on display for everyone to see

Wonder

Jolted heart
marvel in astonishment
Proof of intuition
A state of fascination
Jolted heart
Self curiosity
Over and over again
Reverence for this journey
Souls connected
A luminescent blanket of energetic protection
intertwined connected energy
A journey protected
Jolted heart

Brave

Your still with me gallant
Unflinching courage and sacrifice
To love all of me valiant
Daring through to the truth
My bold love
Strength to climb the walls
To see the robbing of innocence
Mind searching for a place to rest
Landing in tranquility
With ease let go

Silence profound

Stillness I find you in the quietude
a profound whisper a calm
A sudden hush
your soul a lull of peace

Whispers of peace
Calm in the quietude
Lull you into stillness
So profound
Now
Hush

9 789335 721528 2